Am Direct Publishing Complete Guide

Account Opening, Formatting, Cover Design, Publishing, Promotion/Marketing, Get US Payoneer Bank Account to Receive Your Royalties

Steven Bright

Copyright © 2017 Steven Bright

All rights reserved. No part of this publication may be reproduced, stored in a retrieval system, or transmitted in any form or by any means: electronic, photocopying, recording, or mechanical, without the prior written permission of the author.

GETTING STARTED

The era of being rejected by publishing agents or traditional publishers is quite over now. This is because you can now independently publish your manuscript as an eBook, print book as well as hardcover book and get rewarding royalty rates of between (35-70)% as against the meager (15-25)% that most traditional publishers will normally offer you.

Writers and authors can now take advantage of Amazon Kindle Direct Publishing platform to create a successful self-publishing career.

THE POWER OF SELF-PUBLISHING

Do you know that it is a real great freedom and power to be an independent (indie) or self- published author? This is because you are not just the author but also the publisher and marketer of your book.

In fact, your book enjoys some good forms of promotion from Amazon Kindle Direct Publishing through the tools you have access to in your own publishing account bookshelf (free book promotion, Countdown Deal promotion and AMS Ad) to make your books more visible, discoverable and desirable to readers worldwide.

SELF-PUBLISHING SUCCESS TIPS AND GUIDES

Some of the basic things you have to know and do to be successful as an independently published author are enumerated below.

- Write a good book with a well-defined genre in mind.
- Properly edit the manuscript and you can even outsource this task to a professional editor.
- Make use of beta readers to get feedback about the book and your writing.
- Perform the final editing and proofreading of the book.
- Format the manuscript as an eBook with clickable table of content. You can also outsource this to a good eBook formatter.
- Format the book as a print book and hardcover book if you will be offering it in paperbacks and hardcover editions too.
- Design the Cover for the book. You can as well outsource this to a professional graphics designer.
- You should already start marketing the new book to build up buzz for it through word of mouth, social media and online book forums like Goodreads and KBoards.
- Create a publishing account with Amazon kindle Direct Publishing (KDP).
- You can also create an author brand platforms like Facebook author page, Blog, Twitter account or website to promote your author brand and books.
- You can now login to your publishing account on KDP which you created earlier and follow through the processes to publish your book(s).
- You can order a copy once it is live so that you will see what you are offering to readers. This will

help you to be sure that the buyers get a good product and it also gives the book a paid status and sales rank.
- Go to all the available marketing platforms and announce with a post that the book is live. Also tell your friends and family to help create word of mouth buzz for it.
- You can now monitor the performance of your newly published book through the "Report" tab in your publishing account dashboard.
- You should also continue to promote it through social media or any book paid promotion services.
- Congratulations, you are now a published author! But remember that you will need to be consistent in writing and publishing more books because patience and hard-work are needed to be able to profit from self-publishing. That is to say that the more books you write and publish the greater your sales.

It is now time to start working on your next book as soon as possible because the more books you publish, the better the visibility and sales.

.

CONTENTS

Getting Started	i
Strategies for Working on a New Book Project	1
Genres with Great Sales Potentials	5
Formatting Your Book for Publishing using Microsoft Word	6
How to Create a Clickable Table Of Contents (TOC) for an eBook	15
How to Resolve Major Errors in Microsoft Word Formatted Book Manuscript	18
Designing an eBook Cover	20
Designing a Paperback Book Cover	27
Differences Between KDP Account Name and Pen Name	35
Create Kindle Direct Publishing Account	37
Publish Your Book Through Kindle Direct Publishing	38
Getting Your Published eBook URL or Link	43
Book Marketing Strategies	45
Kindle Direct Publishing Promotion Tools	47
Kindle Direct Publishing Sales Report Dashboard	51
How to Open and use Payoneer Bank Account to Receive Payments from KDP	52
How to Enter Your Payoneer Bank Account Details into Your Amazon KDP Account	56
Answers to Some of Your Enquiries	58

STRATEGIES FOR WORKING ON A NEW BOOK PROJECT

As a writer or a traditionally published author who is interested in self-publishing through Amazon Kindle Direct Publishing or any other digital publishing platform, there are things you need to take note of when starting a new book project. I will enumerate some of these things in this section so that you can use it as a check list when working on your next book project.

- Make sure the new book idea fits a worldwide audience.
- If the book project is a series book, ensure you brand the series by selecting a series name that will be short, captivating and marketable. Color theme should also be selected for the covers of all the books in the new series.
- Research the sales potential of the supposed genre of the book idea and see if it is worth it or you will need to optimize it for a different genre. In order to do this, search for books in that genre or sub-genre in the Amazon store and see how they are doing in sales through their sales ranks.
- The next thing is to create an adequate outline for the chapters in the book or sections/scenes.

- You will now have to research any relevant information and resources that will be of help in creating a good content for the book.
- If you have social media followers who are interested in your writing, start building sales momentum for the new book or series. To do this, announce to them the start of the new book or series project and then frequently post about your writing progress on your social media outlets to carry your followers (fans) along.
- Start working on the book cover design if you design your own book covers or hire someone who is competent to start working on it even before you finish the first draft of the book. This gives room for improvement on the original cover design idea for the book and hence getting the best cover design for the new book project at the end of the day.
- Plan and document the launching strategies you will use to promote/market the book. Make sure you use these strategies to give the book a good standing in sales and ranking once it is published.
- Once you complete the writing of the book, get it edited and properly proofread.
- Get the manuscript formatted for eBook, paperback and hardcover book if need be in preparation for publishing. Finalize the cover design for the book too.
- You can now go ahead to publish the book and then start immediately to implement your marketing strategies once the book is "Live" (published).

WRITING GOALS

As a writer and an independent author, it is very important you have a writing goal. This is because you will perform better when you have a desired target to attain. And like in every other endeavor, good and proper goals help you achieve more in short time. This translates to success since the more books you have published through Amazon kindle direct publishing, the greater the chances of making sales since if one title does not sell, there are the chances that another will. So, always have daily, weekly and monthly word count targets, and if possible, the target number of books you want to publish annually.

FICTION AND NONFICTION WRITING TIPS

In reality, the techniques involved in creative writing are not constant but varies from time to time, genre to genre and schools of thought. I'm going to consider this topic from two broad perspectives of fiction and nonfiction writing.

Fiction Writing

The writing of fiction content requires the following skills and many others. Also have it in mind that to get better in writing, you need to read more too most especially good books from the genre of interest and authors you admire.

- Sharp and Organized imagination as fiction writing involves the creation of scenes that are predominantly abstract.
- The ability to properly outline the storyline of the new book project.
- The ability to create compelling and expressive characters. This will make the book a must read

for readers both for your fans and potential new readers.
- The ability to also create dialogues that flows and hence makes the book interesting to the readers.

Nonfiction Writing

The writing of nonfiction content requires the following skills and many others. Like I said earlier, you have to also be an avid reader to be a great writer by reading good books from the authors you admire.

- Nonfiction book writing also requires the ability to adequately outline the storyline of the book.
- It is important to be a good researcher because nonfiction writing involves some facts, real information and a bit of fiction to blend.
- You must have the necessary ability to organize all the information and resources at your disposal to write the desired book.
- Finally, you must creatively write the actual book in a manner that it will be informative, interesting and give a compelling read to the readers.

GENRES WITH GREAT SALES POTENTIALS

It is very good to write to market (already existing audience) ready to buy some particular kinds of books. You need to find out these ripe genres or subgenres and tailor your writings to suit the expectations of the readers.

The best way to discover these genres or subgenres is to research the bestselling books on Amazon and then trace their genres. The following are some genres that are currently selling well on Amazon with respect to whether you are into fiction or nonfiction writing. Also note that your books need to be good, well written, properly edited, and professionally formatted and a good and custom cover designed for it.

Fiction

- Romance
- Erotica
- Science Fiction and Fantasy
- Mystery, Thriller and Suspense.

Nonfiction

- Health and Relationship books
- Food and Weight Management books
- Travel and Tourism books.

FORMATTING YOUR BOOK FOR PUBLISHING USING MICROSOFT WORD

As long as your book is well written and properly formatted and have a good cover designed for it, you will surely get good sales and feedback from readers.

It is very important you know how to create and modify custom styles that you can use to format your manuscript. To create a custom style in Microsoft Word,

- Click the small arrow button under the "Change Styles" tab just to the left of the Styles tab lists of Microsoft Word default styles on the home menu of Word 2010.
- At the bottom of the list, click on the "New Style" button.
- From the dialog box, input the custom style name. From there, you can select its base style, style type; font type, font size and text justification (left, center or right alignment of text). To further customize it, click the drop-down arrow on "Format" at the bottom of the dialog box and click paragraph for instance. In this case, you will be able to set the special first line indent value, line spacing, and "Before and After values" and

then click the OK button so that you will be back on the main dialog box.
- Check the check-box on "Automatically update" so that any update any changes made on this custom style will be automatically updated on all the texts it is applied to on the Microsoft Word document.
- Click the OK button.
- Click on the Home tab, and then click the "Small Arrow" under "Change Styles" and you will see the lists of your custom styles there. You can now select or put the cursor on any part of the manuscript document and click on the appropriate style from the style list to apply it to that part of the document.
- You can also right-click the name of the custom style from the style list and then click on "Modify" from the option list to edit the attributes of the custom style.

FORMATTING AN EBOOK FOR PUBLISHING ON KDP

To format your manuscript as an eBook to a professional standard using Microsoft Word, you will need to make good use of custom styles. The following are the tips to get this done quickly and perfectly.

- Save the manuscript in Microsoft word as a .doc document (Save As 1997-2003) as this publishes fine without any complicated formatting error compared to Microsoft Word default .docx file format.
- Properly edit and proof read as well as removing all tab and space bar spaces. To do this, ON the Show/Hide Microsoft word feature to guide you

(that is click on the last button on the first line of buttons under the "Paragraph" tab in 2010 Microsoft word).
- Create and use custom styles to format the front and end matter of your book. Make sure you center align this style, font size 12, Times New Roman font type.
- Create another custom style for the book content with font size 12, Times New Roman and the alignment should be Justify and set a special first line indent of 0.25". Apply this style to the entire content of the book before you apply any other style.
- Create a custom style for the first paragraph in all the chapters and sections. Set its attributes as in the "body" style but you will have to specify a special first line indent of about 0.01" to trick KDP and prevent it from indenting those paragraphs during publishing such that those first paragraphs will not be indented.
- Create a custom style to format the title of the book with font sizes from anything 18 to 24. Also center align it and bold it and apply it to the title. Create another one to format the subtle but it should not be bold and the font size should be smaller than that of the title of the book.
- Create custom styles to format the main headings and subheadings in the manuscript and set their attributes as stated here: font sizes like 14 and 13 respectively, justify and bold. Also set a special first line indent of 0.01" for them. Apply them to all the headings and subheadings in the book appropriately.
- You can directly apply Bold, Italics, and Underline where necessary.

- Create a Clickable Table of Content for the table of content of the eBook such that clicking on them will take you to that section of the book. There is a section in this book where I will discuss two different methods of doing this.
- Simulate the eBook with your smart phone device or an eBook reader to have a feel of it. If you are convinced it is great, congrats. You can now go ahead to publish it.
- If there are images or illustration in the book. Create a custom style with the following attributes and apply it to the images: "Center align" and the "Before" and "After" values should be at least 8.

Below is a simple structure that shows what an eBook content formatting looks like in practice. Do use it as a guide.

Front Matter:

This is the first page of an eBook. See the sample below.

Title of Book

Subtitle of Book

Steven Bright

Steven Bright

Copyright Steven Bright, 2017

This eBook is licensed for your personal enjoyment only. It may not be re-sold or given away to other people.

Also By Steven Bright:

Name of book one

Name of book three

Name of book four

Table of Contents:

This is the list of all the chapters in an eBook. Some authors will also include section headings too. See the table of contents in this book as a sample.

Body:

This depends on the genre and the choice of the author of the book. It always starts like this:

Introduction

Content………

Chapter 1

Content………

Chapter 2

Content………

Chapter 3

Content.........

Chapter 4

Content.........

Note that fiction eBooks do not always include an introduction chapter.

End Matter:

This is the last page of the eBook and it contains the bibliography of the author. See the example below.

ABOUT THE AUTHOR

Steven Bright is a Tech expert, graphic designer, web developer, eBook formatter, and blogger. He is also the Author of:

> Name of book one
>
> Name of book two
>
> Name of book three
>
> Name of book four

> Connect with "Author Name"
>
> Author Social media outlets or AuthorCentral page

FORMATTING A PRINT BOOK FOR PUBLISHING ON KDP

To format your manuscript as a print book to KDP print standard using Microsoft Word, you will need to make good use of custom styles as well.

The good thing is that such custom styles are already present in Amazon KDP paperback template which you can download by clicking on "Help" from your KDP publishing account and then click on "Paperback formatting. Download the template for the paperback trim size (5"x8" or 6"x9") you want, open it in your computer and paste your manuscript into it. You can then use the styles in the template to format the print book. Make sure you use the appropriate template when formatting a print book (use the 5 inches by 8 inches template for a 5"x8" book trim size and use the 6 inches by 9 inches template for a 6"x9" book trim size).

Click on the Home menu and then click the "Small Arrow" under "Change Styles" and you will see the lists of the custom styles there. Select or put the cursor on any part of the manuscript and apply the appropriate style from the template's style list to it.

Alternatively, you can create your own custom styles like I explained earlier while discussing eBook formatting and then use the styles to format your print book manuscript.

Take note that the number of pages of your paperback formatted book should be a minimum of 72 pages and a minimum of 76 pages for a hardcover formatted book and that the smallest trim size for a paperback book is 5 inches by 8 inches while the smallest trim size for a hardcover book is 5.5 inches by 8.5 inches.

Once you are done with the formatting, you will then need to convert (publish) it as PDF file since that is the document format required by KDP print and hardcover beta. To do this in Microsoft Word 2010,

- Go to File menu.
- Point to "Save AS" and click on the drop-down menu on the "Save as type" and click on "PDF".
- Enter the file name in the "File Name" field.
- Check the "Check box" on "Open the file after Publishing" so that you will preview it.
- Select the Optimize for Standard (Publishing online and printing) option button.
- Click the "Save" button.
- And the Microsoft Word document will be converted to a PDF document which you can now publish on KDP.
- During publishing, one tricky thing is that you will have to click the "Assign Free ISBN Button" to assign KDP print free ISBN to the book if you do not have your own ISBN. You must also preview the uploaded book content using the KDP print online previewer and if you are satisfied, you then click the "Approve" button and you are now taking back to the publishing process to continue. Once on the "Pricing" stage, set the list price for the book using KDP suggested "Minimum and Maximum" prices and the "Printing cost" as guides. After that, you can then click the "Publish button.

These same procedures is what you will use if you are formatting a manuscript for printing as a hardcover book on KDP but the smallest trim size to set it to will be 5.5 inches by 8.5 inches.

You can save you print formatted manuscript as a new document to be used for publishing the hardcover edition of the book but you will have to change its document size to 5.5 inches by 8.5 inches for the smallest hardcover book size on KDP. To do this,

- Go to the "Page Layout" menu.
- Click the drop-down menu on "Margins"
- Go down and click on "Custom Margins"
- From the page setup dialog box, click on "Paper" and then set the width value to 5.5 and the height value to 8.5.
- Go down to where you have "Apply to" and select "Whole document" from the drop-down menu there.
- Click the OK button.

HOW TO CREATE A CLICKABLE TABLE OF CONTENTS (TOC) FOR AN EBOOK

It is a standard for an eBook to have a clickable table of contents so that clicking on an item on the TOC takes a reader to that part of the book and hence makes navigating the eBook easy and seamless. The two main methods used to create a clickable table of contents in Microsoft Word are discussed below.

CREATE TABLE OF CONTENT THROUGH MICROSOFT "INSERT FEATURE"

In this case, you make use of Microsoft Word "table of contents" tool found in the "References Menu" to create a clickable table of content and it is good since you will publish it through Kindle Direct Publishing. To do this, follow these steps.

- Assign Microsoft Word default heading styles ("Heading 1" to chapter headings) and ("Heading 2" or "Heading 3" to section headings) appropriately. To do this, select the heading or subheading text in the book, click on the drop-down menu on the "Styles" tab to reveal the

default Microsoft Word styles options list and then click on "Heading 1" or "Heading 2" to apply it to the selected chapter heading or subheading respectively. Note: make sure you are on the "Home" menu.
- Write a chapter heading "Table of Contents" in the appropriate place in your manuscript where you will place the table of contents list.
- Place the cursor on the point within the document where you want to insert the table of content under the "Table of Contents" heading you created earlier.
- Go to the "Reference" menu and click "Table of Contents".
- Click the "Insert Table of contents" link at the bottom of the dialog box so that you can control the various table of contents options such as showing page numbers, selecting the used heading styles, etc. Once you are through setting all the appropriate options,
- Click the OK button and the clickable table of contents for all the chapter headings and subheadings to which Microsoft Word "Heading 1" or "Heading 2" styles where applied will be automatically used to form a clickable table of contents.

CREATE TABLE OF CONTENTS USING BOOKMARKS AND HYPERLINKS

This is another method of creating a clickable TOC. It is a requirement if you will publish your book through Smashwords as well. The steps below will guide you on the procedures involve.

- Ensure you do not use the default Microsoft word heading styles to format both the chapter and section headings in the book.
- Write a chapter heading "Table of Contents" in the appropriate place in your manuscript where you will place the table of contents list.
- Write a list of chapter headings and subheadings under it.
- You can now create the required Bookmarks. To do this, go to the body of your manuscript and highlight each chapter headings and subheadings if need be that you want to bookmark one after the other and then go to the "Insert" menu and click on "Bookmark" under the "Links" tab. Enter the name of the chapter heading or an abbreviation like C1 for chapter one and click the OK button. Repeat these processes for all the chapter headings and/or subheadings in the book. You will now also go and highlight the "Table of Contents" heading you created earlier and bookmark it with the name "ref_TOC" so that during the conversion processes, the system of your publishing platform will recognize it as the table of contents file heading and converts its list to clickable (working) table of contents.
- The next step is to hyperlink the typed chapter heading lists to their corresponding bookmarks. To do this, highlight each of the chapter heading and then click the "Insert" menu, click on Hyperlink under the "Links" tab, and then select its corresponding bookmark and click the OK button. Repeat these processes to hyperlink all the chapter headings to their corresponding bookmarks.

HOW TO RESOLVE MAJOR ERRORS IN MICROSOFT WORD FORMATTED BOOK MANUSCRIPT

At times, the formatting of the content of a book whether it is an eBook or print book may be bad and an author needs to reformat the book. To be able to do this correctly, a clean manuscript of the book without any form of formatting is required and to get this from the wacked formatted book manuscript, you have to go nuclear with your already formatted book. The steps to do this are as follows:

- Copy and paste the entire content of the book into Notepad to get rid of all the previous formatting. Notepad software is always preinstalled in most operating systems. So, you most likely have it in your computer. Just type Notepad into your operating system search tool to search for and open it.
- Open the Microsoft word document for your book manuscript, select all its content using Ctrl+A and use Ctrl+C to copy all the content of the formatted book.
- Paste it into the opened Notepad software.

- Select all its content using Ctrl+A on the Notepad software and use Ctrl+C to copy all of it.
- Open a new Microsoft Word document and paste it there.
- Save it now as a new Microsoft Word file to get a clean manuscript of your book again.
- Reformat the clean manuscript of your book to your taste. Do make use of custom styles to properly format it this time around.
- You can now sign-in to your publishing account to publish or republish the book.

DESIGNING AN EBOOK COVER

The first thing you should know about cover design is that it is the first part of the book the potential buyer have contact with and that means it will determine if the sales will go through or not. The following tips will be helpful to you while designing cover for an eBook.

- It should portray the genre of the eBook, its title and theme.
- It should be great but simple in design and should not be clustered with too many details.
- Take a look at best sellers' eBook cover designs in your genre of interest to learn from them.
- It should be clean and clear even as a thumbnail.
- Choose your design colors wisely.
- You need a basic know-how of CorelDRAW, Photoshop or any other graphics design software to be able to design custom made covers for an eBooks all by yourself.
- It should be an upright rectangle and exported as a JPEG file with its size in the range of 1600 by 2560 pixels (Width by Height).
- You can also contract the design out to a professional eBook cover designer if need be.

When you are through with the design of the eBook cover, export it as a JPEG or JPG file and set its color mode to RGB during the file export processes. You can do this by using the shortcut keys Ctrl+E in CorelDraw and then set the "Save as type" to JPEG or JPG and the size to the range stated above in pixels.

You may like my book on how to learn and perfect your CorelDRAW skills through a step by step guide, which is also live on Amazon. Its title on Amazon is "CorelDraw How: The Fundamental of CorelDRAW"

The illustrations below are my eBook cover designs for some of my books using CorelDraw.

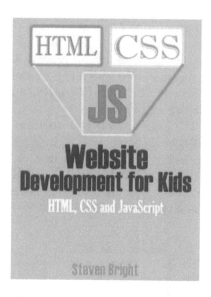

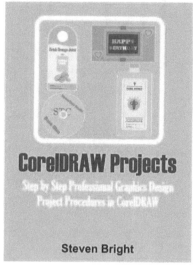

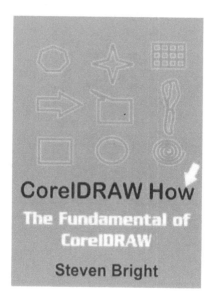

DESIGNING A PAPERBACK BOOK COVER

The following tips and analysis will be of great help to you while designing cover for your Kindle Direct Publishing print book.

- You need to take note of the trim size of the formatted paperback book. That is whether it is 5 by 8 inches or 6 by 9 inches in size. Note the Trim line is represented by the dotted line in the illustrated diagram below.
- Spine width size is calculated as 0.002252 multiplied by the Number of pages in the paperback formatted content of the book.
- Width of the paperback book cover is bleed + front cover + spine + back cover + bleed. Which means 0.25+5+spine value+5+0.25 for 5 inches by 8 inches paperback book cover (5 inches is the front cover and back cover trim sizes and 8 inches is the height trim size).
- Height of the paperback book cover is 0.25+8+0.25.
- Note that Barcode code area is 0.25 inches from both trim line and spine margin. You must make

sure you do not place any printable text or image on this area.

- For spine Text, make sure you observe the spine text margin of 0.0625inches. This implies that for a spine of 0.800 inches, the spine Text width will be 0.800 - (0.0625x2) = 0.675 inches. Also note that spine Text size is only relevant if the number of pages in the book is at least 100 and text can then be placed on the spine of the book cover.

The illustration below is a dimension analysis that shows how a paperback cover design is structured.

Note that the values in the analysis above are in inches and that 0.25 is the bleed. The number of pages of your paperback formatted book should be a minimum of 72 pages and a minimum of 76 pages for a hardcover formatted book. Also, the smallest trim size for a paperback book is 5 inches by 8 inches while the smallest trim size for a hardcover book is 5.5 inches by 8.5 inches.

This implies total paperback book cover width size is its front cover plus the spine plus the back cover. The spine is always at the center of the paperback book cover.

PARAMETER CALCULATIONS

The following are the parameters you will calculate and then use to design a paperback print cover in CorelDraw.

- Spine Width = Number of pages times 0.002252 (spine width multiplier).
- Cover Width = Margin + Trim width + Spine + Trim width + Margin.
- Cover Height = Margin + Trim height + Margin.

As a graphics designer, I prefer doing my print book cover design using CorelDraw. I will then convert it to a Photoshop file by using the export feature in CorelDraw or use the shortcut keys Ctrl+E and then set the "Save as type" to PSD during the file export processes and its color mode to CYMK. I will then open the file using the Photoshop software and use the "Save As" features in the "File" menu in Photoshop to save it as a PDF file. It is also important to set its "Average down-sampling to 300 DPI through the "Compression tab to the left of the "Save As" dialog box in Photoshop.

During publishing, you can set the cover finish to "Glossy" which is suitable for nonfiction, book and children books. Otherwise, you can set it to matte which is suitable for fiction books.

Note that KDP Print beta cover creator is an alternative to custom book cover upload option and many Indie authors also make use of it.

For Hardcover book cover design, the procedures are similar to the one described here but you will do the parameter calculations by using the "KDP Cover Calculator" which you can find on the KDP help pages on their website. While there, input the details for the book into the appropriate fields or select the appropriate option from the option list in the cover calculator e.g. binding type, interior type, paper type, interior trim size, page count, page turn direction, etc and then click the "Calculate dimensions" button. Once the result of the dimension calculation comes out, get all the necessary values from it on that page and use them in your hardcover book cover design.

The illustrations below are my paperback book cover designs for some of my books using CorelDraw.

Amazon Kindle Direct Publishing Complete Guide

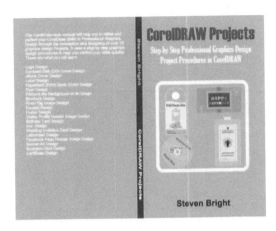

Steven Bright

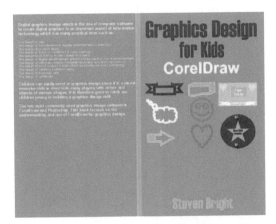

Steven Bright

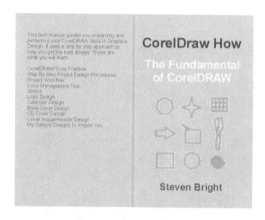

DIFFERENCES BETWEEN KDP ACCOUNT NAME AND PEN NAME

KINDLE DIRECT PUBLISHING ACCOUNT NAME

Your Kindle Direct Publishing account name is your real name or legal name which you used in creating your Kindle Direct Publishing account. It must be the name in your official document as it is expected to be the same name in the account number which you will use to collect your royalties via Electronic Fund Transfer (EFT). Hence, it is the same name you will use to register for Payoneer bank account later if you need it.

PEN NAME

This is an author name in his book other than his legal or real name. An author is allowed to publish a book under a name other than his/her legal title through his Kindle Direct Publishing account.

Note that the author name in any of your book can be your real name or a pen name but the author name in any particular book must be consistently used in the following parts of the book.

- The name on the book cover.
- The name in the front matter (front page).
- The name in the end matter (About the Author).
- The "Author name" field during publishing of the book.

CREATE KINDLE DIRECT PUBLISHING ACCOUNT

To self-publish your books through Kindle Direct Publishing, you need to open and set up a publisher account with KDP. To do this,

- Go to https://kdp.amazon.com/
- Click the sign up button.
- Enter your email and click the option button that says "You are a new customer".
- You will be taken to the registration page.
- Fill the registration form with the required details.
- Click the create account button.
- Your account is now live. Continue its setup by providing other necessary details in your account area of the dashboard.
- You can now take the tax interview.
- Go ahead and publish your book(s) through your KDP account.
- Add your bank account details to your KDP account so you can get your royalties through Electronic Fund Transfer (EFT). See the last chapter for the full procedures on how to do this.

PUBLISH YOUR BOOK THROUGH KINDLE DIRECT PUBLISHING

To publish your book through you Kindle Direct Publishing account, follow the steps in this section. Do make sure you have formatted the book for publishing and designed a good cover for it too.

- Login to your Kindle Direct Publishing account.
- Under "Create a New Title" click the button "Kindle eBook" to publish it as an eBook. To publish it as a paperback book or Hardcover book, click on the respective "Paperback" or "Hardcover" button.
- Follow through the processes to publish it by entering all the details of the book until you get to the "Pricing Page" and then click the publish button to publish the book. See figures 1 and 2 below for further guide.
- After about 24 hours, the book will be successfully published (Live) and you can spread the news of your book being live on Amazon either through social media or word of mouth.
- Start implementing your planned promotional strategies.

- You can also buy a copy of your book so that you will be able to testify that it is in perfect format after publishing to ensure buyers are getting a good product. The royalties also comes back to you and it also quickly give the book a "paid" status and rank and hence more visibility/greater chance of sales success.
- Also login in with your Kindle Direct Publishing details to Authorcentral.com and create an account. Claim your books using their ASIN. Also setup your AuthorCentral author page so that your followers will get to know you better by uploading your author Avatar, write your bibliography and feed your blog or website posts to your AuthorCentral page.

Royalty rates are either 35% or 75% (which applies to books with a list price of $2.99 and above). Note that the price for your book should be determined by the quality of the information and number of pages in the book. Also choose your price wisely and not set it too high to avoid scaring away potential buyers.

Figure 1

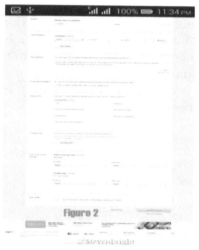

Figure 2

Below is a screenshot of what author central page of an author looks like. From the image, you can see the authors' avatar (Picture), bibliography, page URL and Website feeds.

THE PUBLISHING PROCESSES DETAILED PROCEDURES EXPLAINED

The main steps involved in book publishing through your Kindle Direct Publishing account are as follows.

- Once you login to your Kindle Direct Publishing account, click on "Kindle eBook" to publish your book as an eBook and start to fill the forms with the required information.
- During publishing, in the first stage there is a button to upload your eBook content (formatted manuscript) and a button to upload the eBook cover. Just click on that button and navigate to where it is on your device to pick it up. As for the cover, under cover upload, first select the option button that says "upload already made eBook cover" and you can then click the cover upload button to upload the cover just like you did for the eBook content earlier.

- Also make sure you select the copyright option button that says you "You own the copyright".
- In the description box, you enter the description or summary (blurb) for your eBook.
- In the "Keywords fields", you enter words or phrases that you think a buyer looking for a book like yours will use to search for it on Amazon.
- On the "Category field", click on category, select "Nonfiction" if you book is a nonfiction book or "Fiction" if it is a fiction book. You can then choose or select two categories from the lists that you think your book belongs to and then click the "Save" button.
- On the third stage, make sure you check the box on top of that page to enroll the book in the "Kindle Select" program which can give your book better visibility and also for you to earn more royalties from pages read in addition to the direct sales of the book. Only check the "Kindle Select Enrollment Box" to enroll it in the select program only if you are sure you will not publish the book as an eBook through any other digital book publishing platform or distributor.
- Enter the list price for the book in the price field and then click the "Publish" button at the bottom of the page.

Note that these procedures for publishing your manuscript as an eBook through KDP are similar to the once you will also need to follow when publishing it as a paperback or hardcover book except where you will have to click a button to ask KDP to assign a free ISBN to the print book or to compulsorily preview the print book before it will be published.

GETTING YOUR PUBLISHED EBOOK's URL OR LINK

You will need to get the link or URL of your published book's because it is what you will use to promote or market it to direct readers or potential buyers to the book's sales page on Amazon.

- Once your book is "Live" that is when its status changes from "In Review" to "Publishing" and finally to "Live" which means it is successfully published, it can now be purchased through Amazon digital stores and you can add it to your AuthorCentral account book list too and it will be added in about ten minutes to one hour later.
- You can then click on the book on your AuthorCentral account to go to its Amazon sales page using the "View on Amazon" button. Once you are on its sales page on Amazon, you will see its link or URL displayed on the browser URL field. Copy it from there and that is the link for the book which you can use to promote it on social media or your website. That link is the book's .com URL (That is Amazon USA market).
- Alternatively, you can copy the url for one of my books below and just copy the ASIN number for your book from your KDP dashboard and select

the one on the link and paste in yours to get the .com market link of your book.

https://www.amazon.com/dp/B088ZX1WS8

- Repeat the above processes to get the url for other amazon market places for your published books using the links below as a template.

https://www.amazon.co.uk/dp/B088ZX1WS8
https://www.amazon.ca/dp/B088ZX1WS8
https://www.amazon.com.au/dp/B088ZX1WS8

BOOK MARKETING STRATEGIES

In developing a marketing or promotion strategies for your books, you have to take note of the following most especially if you want to avoid unusually high book sales return of some of the sales you made as an independent author.

- Your book should be good enough to satisfy buyers/readers. So, make sure your book content is of high quality and it meets the expectations of the target audience.
- Your book should be properly formatted. So, make sure the formatting of your book content is good and that is well organized.
- Your book cover design should be suitable! That is it should depict the genre of the book and convey the theme and message you are passing to readers.
- Your book should be listed in the appropriate categories with appropriate keywords during the publishing processes. This will make sure the right audience finds the book.
- If your writing and book meet the above expectations, then there will be minimal return of your book sales and it will also get positive reviews.

- Also, use good and appropriate keywords that will complement the categories to increase the visibility of your book.
- The blurb or description of the book must be great and converting such that it leads potential readers to click through the buy button.
- You need to plan the launch of your new books. This might include self-promotional strategies like (cover reveal events, beta reading groups, pre-order, social media posts, blog or website posts etc.) or paid new book launching promotional services.

KINDLE DIRECT PUBLISHING PROMOTION TOOLS

The following are the various Kindle Direct Publishing (KDP) promotional tools which you can use to promote and market your books.

FREE BOOK DEAL

Free book promotion is used to make your book temporary available at $0.00 price so that people can buy it for free. A book is only qualified for this promotional feature only if it is enrolled in the "Kindle Select" program.

Note that any eBook enrolled in the "Kindle select" program must be published exclusively on Amazon that is to say that you are not allowed to publish it through any other eBook publishing platform during the period of its enrollment which usually lasts for three months.

It helps to create visibility for your book and author brand. This is because some of the people who downloaded one of your books when it was free can like your writing and decide to buy your other books. They therefore become your fan and also help to spread the word about you and your books.

This tool work best for series books or any other related titles that can make a reader buy the other books after reading the free book offer and liked it. It is therefore important that you have a back-list before you ever use the free promotion deal. This means you should never give your only and first title out for free except it is just a novella to test the waters for a new pen name. To use this promotional tool to give out your book for free, follow these steps:

- Login to your Kindle Direct Publishing account.
- Click on the "Promote" button to the right of the book on your bookshelf.
- Select or check the radio button for "free book promotion" under "Run a price promotion"
- Set the start and ending days (maximum of 5).
- Click the save button.
- You can then use book promotion services to expand the reach of the free book promotion or your social media outlets like Facebook groups, Twitter, author website or mailing list to get more visibility and many downloads on the days of the free promotion of the book.

KINDLE COUNTDOWN DEAL

Countdown Deal book promotion is used to make your book available at a lower price than the actual list price. A book is only qualified for this promotional feature if it is also enrolled in the "Kindle Select" program.

Kindle Countdown Deal promotion is a better alternative to Kindle Direct Publishing free promotion Deal feature once your eBook has a list price that meets the following price criteria:

$2.99-$24.99 on (Amazondotcom) and £1.99-£15.99 on (Amazondotcodotuk)

Note that you will still get 70% royalty from Kindle Countdown Deal sales even if the promotional price is less than $2.99.

The countdown Deal only runs on the above two Amazon national markets. But you must make sure you promote the Countdown Deal book to get a better result. To use this promotional tool to give out your book at a lower price, follow these steps:

- Login to your KDP account.
- Click on the "Promote" button to the right of the book on your bookshelf.
- Check the radio button for "Kindle Countdown Deal" under "Run a price promotion".
- Set the start and ending days (maximum of 7).
- Set the price reduction range.
- Click the save button.
- Makes sure you setup the Countdown Deal to run simultaneously on both Amazon US and UK markets.
- You can then use book promotion services to expand the reach of the Countdown Deal book or use your social media outlets like Facebook groups, Twitter, author website, or mailing list to get more visibility and sales on the days of the promotion of the book.

AMAZON MARKETING SERVICES (AMS)

This is Amazon's in-house marketing services. It is a Paid service and you have to create an AMS account with a $100 minimum budget which you can then use to create an AMS Ad for any of your books. To use AMS to market any of your books, follow these steps:

- Login to your KDP account.
- Click on the "Promote" button to the right of the book on your bookshelf.
- Click on "Create an Ad Campaign" under "Run an Ad Campaign".
- Follow through the entire process to create the Ad.
- Note that you have to monitor the Ad to know how it is performing with respect to impressions, clicks, and sales to now if you are fine with it or you want to tweak its keywords or to stop it.

KINDLE DIRECT PUBLISHING SALES REPORT DASHBOARD

A click on the "Reports" tab on the top of your account automatically takes you to the sales report dashboard where you will find two charts and the list of royalties earned by market places for the current month. The first chart is for "Units Ordered" With the introduction of the Kindle Direct Publishing print and Hardcover book beta, this chart now contains four components that is Paid units (eBook) "in orange" color, Free units eBook "in blue" color, Paid units (Paperback) :in grey" color and Paid units (Hardcover) :in red" color.

The second chart is the Kindle Edition Normalized Pages (KENP) read chart. This displays the number of pages read for your eBooks enrolled in the kindle select program. Note that the actual royalty report for pages read comes with the monthly sales report which you can download and analyze.

The third component of the sales dashboard is the regular "ordered units" royalties listed by market places. Note that what you have here may at times differ from the reports of the "ordered units" chart. This is usually due to refunds or orders that are yet to be cleared. It is therefore safer to click the "Generate Report" button at the bottom of the page to view the actual royalties earned data for the period. Also note that as a day fall off the ordered units chart to accommodate a new date, the royalties for the previous day also falls off the royalties report list.

HOW TO OPEN AND USE PAYONEER BANK ACCOUNT TO RECEIVE PAYMENTS FROM KDP

Payoneer is a payment solution that is very friendly with those countries whose banks are not accepted by Amazon Kindle Direct Publishing. With Payoneer, you will be able to open and own a U.S bank account as a Non-U.S citizen with which you can receive payments from some online businesses you work with. It is a checking account and you are provided with a master card with which you can use the money to buy things online or withdraw the fund through any ATM that accepts master card.

This implies that you will no longer wait to accumulate royalties or earnings from your online businesses to a certain threshold before you get paid by check (cheque) which always comes with some challenges like undelivered checks, high cost of clearing it or being unable to clear a check.

REGISTER AND APPLY FOR PAYONEER BANK ACCOUNT

You can apply for the Payoneer Bank account for free by going to the company's website:
https://www.payoneer.com/

Once you successfully register, you will receive an email informing you of the approval. Make sure you use your legal details same with the ones used in your online businesses account. The next email you will receive from them will contain your bank account details like (The name of the Bank, account number, routing number, and your holder name). To register and open the Payoneer bank account, follow the steps below:

- Go to Payoneer website https://www.payoneer.com/
- Fill the form provided with the required details.
- Make sure you use a correct P.O. Box mailing address (quite more reliable) or postal code, house address, email, and phone number.
- You will receive an approval email and account details through your email soon after registration.
- In one of the emails you will be informed that your Payoneer card have been shipped through regular mail and the expected period of delivery.
- From experience, the regular mail delivery is not too effective because the expected delivery period may pass without you receiving the Payoneer master card. So, in such a case, login to your Payoneer account and re-order the card but ask them to ship it through expedited shipping if you want.

SUBMIT THE REQUIRED DOCUMENTS

After successfully opening the account and while you await the delivery of the card, it is good you login to your Payoneer account using your email and password to submit the verification documents. At the bottom of the page, click on the button that ask you to submit evidence of your online business and identity card. Properly submit these documents.

You can now go to your online business accounts and enter your Payoneer bank details appropriately. Make sure you select EFT as the payment option and checking as type of bank account.

RE-ORDER PAYONEER CARD

If after almost two months of application your card was not delivered by regular mail, then it is good you login to your Payoneer account to re-order it and then let them deliver it through expedited shipping via DHL which will cost you $40 and the card will be delivered to you in few days. The delivery cost will be taken from your Payoneer card and this was why I advised you enter the account details into your online businesses account so that you will start receiving payments into it.

ACTIVATE YOUR PAYONEER CARD

Once you receive your Payoneer card, the next step is to login to your Payoneer account profile on their website and activate it. To do this, follow these steps:

- Login to your Payoneer account.
- Click on the "Activate" tab at the top of the dashboard.
- Enter the card number in the field provided for it.
- Enter your chosen PIN in the field provided for it.
- Confirm the PIN by entering it again in the next field.
- Click the OK button.

- Your Payoneer card is now activated and ready for use.

CHECK ACCOUNT BALANCE OR WITHDRAW CASH

You can check your account balance by login in to your Payoneer profile on the company's website and you will see your account balance or through an Automated Teller Machine (ATM) and the balance in this case will be displayed in your local currency. Note that this second option of checking account balance costs you one dollar any time you use it.

As for cash withdrawal from your Payoneer account, you can use any ATM that accepts master card to withdraw money from your account in your local currency. You will be charged $3.15 per withdraw irrespective of the amount withdrawn. Alternatively, you can connect your local bank account to your Payoneer bank account and then use the "withdraw to bank" option through the Payoneer website to withdraw your funds into your local bank account.

HOW TO ENTER YOUR PAYONEER BANK ACCOUNT DETAILS INTO YOUR AMAZON KDP ACCOUNT

It is very important you know how to connect your Payoneer bank account to your Kindle Direct Publishing account.

You will first need to get your Payoneer bank account details from the Payoneer website. To do this,

- Login to Payoneer website with the details you used for registering with them.
- Click on Global Services.
- From there, you will see your bank account name, bank name, account number and the routing number. All these details are what you need.

The procedures for entering your Payoneer bank account details into your Kindle Direct Publishing account are described below.

- Login to your Kindle Direct Publishing account.
- Scroll down to just after the tax interview and click on the link "Add Bank".
- Select the country from the option list there. This should be US since Payoneer bank account is

provided by a US bank. Except you are using any of the other bank account alternatives from other countries Payoneer provided for you and in that case you fill in the appropriate details correctly for that bank account.

- Enter the bank name, account number, routing number and your name as the holder in the fields provided for them and select checking as the type of account. This will automatically be added to all Amazon's national market places.
- Click on the + sign in front of each market place to confirm that Electronic Fund Transfer (EFT) payment option is selected and also set the currency of your choice.
- You will now start receiving royalties for your book sales from Amazon KDP into your Payoneer bank account.

ANSWERS TO SOME OF YOUR ENQUIRIES

ON HOW KDP WORKS

You write the manuscript of your book, edit and proofread it, format it and design a professional book cover for it. You then create a publishing account with Amazon KDP and publish the book. You are paid Royalties on each unit sales of the book. There are two types of royalties 35% and 70% of the list price.

ON EBOOK PAGE NUMBERING

There might be page numbers in your eBook formatted manuscript for publishing on kindle but it is not necessary because an eBook is reflow-able that is the page numbers are not static but depends on the size of the device a reader is using to read it. Hence a particular book will have more pages in a smaller screen device than it does on a bigger screen device. For this reason, it is not necessary to insert page numbers in an eBook formatted manuscript.

ON PAPERBACK BOOK AND HARDCOVER BOOK NUMBER OF PAGES

The number of pages of your paperback book formatted manuscript should be a minimum of 72 and a minimum of 76 pages for a hardcover book formatted manuscript.

ON PAPERBACK BOOK AND HARDCOVER BOOK MINIMUM TRIM SIZES

The smallest trim size for a paperback book formatted manuscript is 5 inches by 8 inches while the smallest trim size for a hardcover book formatted manuscript is 5.5 inches by 8.5 inches.

ON ISBN

It is not compulsory to buy you own ISBN if you are publishing books through Amazon Kindle Direct Publishing since they can provide for your eBooks their own catalog number called ASIN as well as a free ISBN for your print books.

ON KEYWORDS

Authors and writers always want to know how they can get appropriate keywords to use when publishing their books through Kindle Direct Publishing. To get your keywords right, you need to have an understanding of search engine optimization. The simple way to do this is to put yourself in the place of a potential buyer and imagine what appropriate words (keywords) you will use to searching for the book if you were searching for such a book on Amazon or on the internet generally.

ON KDP PAYMENT NOTIFICATION BUT THERE IS NOTHING IN MY PAYONEER BANK ACCOUNT!

It is just a notification of payments to be made, which comes at the middle of every month. The actual payments are not made until anything from on the 28th day and above of every month. So, at the end of the month you will definitely receive your royalty payments into your bank account.

ON HOW TO BECOME A PROFICIENT WRITER

The following steps will be of great help to you in your desire to improve your writing and become a proficient and successful writer.

- Read good books in the genre you are interested in for toy to understand the basic structure and themes used by established authors whose books you are reading. Also put into consideration your purpose of writing and be passionate about it.
- Learn and perfect how to express your thought through outlining of book ideas.
- Make sure you write every day and your writing will improve as you do.
- Acquire basic editing and proofreading skills. This will help to sharpen your writing style.
- Make sure you get feedbacks on your writing by sharing it with people most especially other writers.

ON BEST NICHES

I personally don't go after niches. So I can't give an exact answer on this. One thing I can say is for you to write in different niches to see which one picks up for you and then focus more on that genre. For example, you can try out romance, mystery and young adults and then settle on any of the three that gives you the best return.

ON WHAT IT WILL COST ME TO PUBLISH MY BOOK

On the aspect of Amazon Kindle Direct Publishing, it will cost you nothing to publish your book through them as they earn a percentage of each sales of your book just like you will earn royalties which is also a percentage of each sales of the book. The areas you will have to spend is in formatting your manuscript for publishing, designing book cover for the book and in marketing it once it is published.

ON FREE EBOOK PROMOTION

To use Amazon's free book promotion to promote any of your KDP published books, click on the "Promote and Advertise" button to the right of the book on your bookshelf. Select the option button on "Free book Promotion" and click the orange button there to create the free promotion Ad by following through the processes to setup the free promotion. On the day of the free promotion, do make sure you use social media, your email list or a paid advert to get the word out about it.

ON COUNTDOWN DEAL PROMOTION

Countdown deal is a KDP marketing tool that allows authors to reduce the price of their books for a seven days promo and still get 70% royalties of each unit sales of the book. To do this, click on the "Promote and Advertise" button to the right of the book on your bookshelf. Select the option button on "Countdown Deal Promotion" and click the orange button there to start the Countdown Deal Promotion by following through the processes to setup the Countdown Deal promotion. On the day of the Countdown deal promotion, do make sure you use social media, your email list or a paid advert to get the word out about it.

ON "KINDLE SELECT" PROGRAM

You can enroll your book in the KDP "Kindle Select" program during the publishing processes on Amazon KDP by checking the "Kindle Select" enrolment checkbox on the third stage of the publishing processes. Does this affect your earnings? Yes and No. Yes because it is another way readers buy your book that is those who have Amazon subscription download books enrolled in the "Kindle Select" program and the authors are paid some few cents per pages read. No because this does not work for all authors or books as some authors earn most of their royalties from direct book sales.

ABOUT THE AUTHOR

Steven Bright is an Engineer, Tech expert, Graphics designer, Web developer, eBook formatter, and Blogger. He is also the Author of:

1. JavaScript Fundamentals: JavaScript Syntax, What JavaScript is Use for in Website Development, JavaScript Variable, Strings, Popup Boxes, JavaScript Objects, Function, and Event Handlers.

2. Photoshop Beginner Guide: Photoshop Tools and their Functions, Photoshop Tools Practice, Color Management, File Formats, Photography, and Graphics Design.

3. CorelDraw How: The Fundamental of CorelDRAW.

4. Tools and Function Lists: Engineering Tools Manual.

5. Microsoft Word: Customizing the Quick Access Toolbar, Equations, Underline Styles, Insert Menu, Table, Page Layout, Formatting a Document, Edit Manuscript, and Preparation of an eBook for Publishing.

6. Microsoft Office Productivity Pack: Microsoft Excel, Microsoft Word, and Microsoft PowerPoint.

7. Computer Fundamentals: Introduction to Computer, Uses of Computer, Main Components of Computer, Input/Output Devices, Hardware/Software, Operating System, Internet, and More.

8. Microsoft PowerPoint: Creating a Presentation, Tips for Creating and Delivering an Effective Presentation, and Marketing Your Brand through PowerPoint Presentation.

9. Microsoft Excel: Microsoft Excel User Interface, Excel Basics, Function, Database, Financial Analysis, Matrix, Statistical Analysis.

10. Master Cascading Style Sheets (CSS) Quickly: CSS Properties, CSS Property Definitions, Inline CSS, Internal CSS, External CSS and Sample Codes.

11. The ABC of eBook Publishing: Kindle Direct Publishing, Draft2Digital, Smashwords, Writing, Formatting, Creating an Active Table of Content, and Marketing Guide.

12. Windows Operating System: Windows Operating System (OS) Installation, Basic Windows OS Operations, Disk Defragment, Disk Partitioning, Windows OS Upgrade, System Restore, and Disk Formatting.

13. Facebook Groups for Authors: How to Use Facebook Author and Book Promotion Groups to Generate Sales and Create Visibility for Your Books.

Made in United States
Troutdale, OR
09/21/2024